GUIDANCE &
GOD'S WILL

11 Studies for Individuals or Groups
T O M & J O A N S T A R K

Harold Shaw Publishers • Wheaton, Illinois

ISBN 0-87788-324-6

99   98   97   96

15   14   13   12

CONTENTS

INTRODUCTION

Have you noticed that life's decisions don't seem to get easier—only more complex? On top of the "big" choices of where to go to college, who to marry, and what career to pursue, there are endless smaller decisions every day. And then along comes a new barrage of big choices again with ever-widening repercussions.

As followers of Jesus, we want to make godly decisions that reflect the values of his kingdom. How can we make those kinds of choices?

The idea of knowing God's will has more to do with understanding principles than with tracking down specific information. Although the Holy Spirit does guide us specifically in prayer and we arrive at specific answers through meditation and counsel, the Bible itself gives more general guidelines. Knowing God's will is often more a matter of daily obedience to what we know in God's Word than flashes of unusual direction.

The following studies affirm supernatural guidance and intervention as well as the more "unexciting" ways of finding wisdom, such as Bible study, common sense, and seeking the counsel of competent advisers. We tend to remember miracles, but the Bible is also filled with instances of very pragmatic and uneventful decision-making. The excitement comes in knowing that God's will is "good, pleasing and perfect." As he has led in the past, he will continue to lead in the future.

HOW TO USE THIS STUDYGUIDE

Fisherman studyguides are based on the inductive approach to Bible study. Inductive study is discovery study; we discover what the Bible says as we ask questions about its content and search for answers. This is quite different from the process in which a teacher *tells* a group *about* the Bible and what it means and what to do about it. In inductive study God speaks directly to each of us through his Word.

A group functions best when a leader keeps the discussion on target, but this leader is neither the teacher nor the "answer person." A leader's responsibility is to *ask*—not *tell*. The answers come from the text itself as group members examine, discuss, and think together about the passage.

There are four kinds of questions in each study. The first is an *approach question*. Used before the Bible passage is read, this question breaks the ice and helps you focus on the topic of the Bible study. It begins to reveal where thoughts and feelings need to be transformed by Scripture.

Some of the earlier questions in each study are *observation questions* designed to help you find out basic facts—who, what, where, when, and how.

When you know what the Bible says you need to ask, *What does it mean?* These *interpretation questions* help you to discover the writer's basic message.

Application questions ask, *What does it mean to me?* They challenge you to live out the Scripture's life-transforming message.

Fisherman studyguides provide spaces between questions for jotting down responses and related questions you would like to raise in the group. Each group member should have a copy of the studyguide and may take a turn in leading the group.

A group should use any accurate, modern translation of the Bible such as the *New International Version,* the *New American Standard Bible,* the *Revised Standard Version,* the *New Jerusalem Bible,* or the *Good News Bible.* (Other translations or paraphrases of the Bible may be referred to when additional help is needed.) Bible commentaries should not be brought to a Bible study because they tend to dampen discussion and keep people from thinking for themselves.

SUGGESTIONS FOR GROUP LEADERS

1. Read and study the Bible passage thoroughly beforehand, grasping its themes and applying its teachings for yourself. Pray that the Holy Spirit will "guide you into truth" so that your leadership will guide others.

2. If the studyguide's questions ever seem ambiguous or unnatural to you, rephrase them, feeling free to add others that seem necessary to bring out the meaning of a verse.

3. Begin (and end) the study promptly. Start by asking someone to pray for God's help. Remember, the Holy Spirit is the teacher, not you!

4. Ask for volunteers to read the passages out loud.

5. As you ask the studyguide's questions in sequence, encourage everyone to participate in the discussion. If some are silent, ask, "What do you think, Heather?" or, "Dan, what can you add to that answer?" or suggest, "Let's have an answer from someone who hasn't spoken up yet."

6. If a question comes up that you can't answer, don't be afraid to admit that you're baffled! Assign the topic as a research project for someone to report on next week.

7. Keep the discussion moving and focused. Though tangents will inevitably be introduced, you can bring the discussion back to the topic at hand. Learn to pace the discussion so that you finish a study each session you meet.

8. Don't be afraid of silences: some questions take time to answer and some people need time to gather courage to speak. If silence persists, rephrase your question, but resist the temptation to answer it yourself.

9. If someone comes up with an answer that is clearly illogical or unbiblical, ask him or her for further clarification: "What verse suggests that to you?"

10. Discourage Bible-hopping and overuse of cross-references. Learn all you can from *this* passage, along with a few important references suggested in the studyguide.

11. Some questions are marked with a ♦. This indicates that further information is available in the Leader's Notes at the back of the guide.

12. For further information on getting a new Bible study group started and keeping it functioning effectively, read Gladys Hunt's *You Can Start a Bible Study Group* and *Pilgrims in Progress: Growing through Groups* by Jim and Carol Plueddemann.

SUGGESTIONS FOR GROUP MEMBERS

1. Learn and apply the following ground rules for effective Bible study. (If new members join the group later, review these guidelines with the whole group.)

2. Remember that your goal is to learn all that you can *from the Bible passage being studied*. Let it speak for itself without using Bible commentaries or other Bible passages. There is more than enough in each assigned passage to keep your group productively occupied for one session. Sticking to the passage saves the group from insecurity and confusion.

3. Avoid the temptation to bring up those fascinating tangents that don't really grow out of the passage you are discussing. If the topic is of common interest, you can bring it up later in informal conversation following the study. Meanwhile, help each other stick to the subject!

4. Encourage each other to participate. People remember best what they discover and verbalize for themselves. Some people are naturally shyer than others, or they may be afraid of making a mistake. If your discussion is free and friendly and you show real interest in what other group members think and feel, they will be more likely to speak up. Remember, the more people involved in a discussion, the richer it will be.

5. Guard yourself from answering too many questions or talking too much. Give others a chance to express themselves. If you are one who participates easily, discipline yourself by counting to ten before you open your mouth!

6. Make personal, honest applications and commit yourself to letting God's Word change you.

THE BASIS FOR KNOWING GOD'S WILL

Romans 12:1-2; 2 Corinthians 3:13-18

Someone has said, "The only important decision we have to make is to live with God. He will make the rest."

What does it mean "to live with God"? In his letter to Christians in Rome, the apostle Paul outlines the foundations of our faith: how we are redeemed and how we should continue to live as redeemed persons. Romans 12 then discusses the practical outworking of this theology in individual lives.

1. What do you consider to be your purpose in life?

Read Romans 12:1-2.

2. These verses contain three instructions. Paraphrase
them in your own words.

— body as living sacrifice
— do not conform to this
  world
— be transformed by
  renewal of mind

◆ **3.** What is Paul's basis for giving his readers these
instructions?

4. What does Paul say will be the result of carrying out
these instructions? What difference would it make in a
Christian's life to experience this result?

5. What does the term "present your body" to Christ mean? How would you do this?

6. What are the characteristics of "the world"? In what areas do you find yourself tempted to conform to it? Give specific examples.

♦ **7.** What words does Paul use to describe God's will? How does this description coincide with *your* expectations of God's will?

Read 2 Corinthians 3:13-18.

◆ **8.** These verses refer to the new covenant—the new way
ushered in by the life, death, and resurrection of Christ.
God's plan for us is no longer hidden and given to only a
chosen few, like Moses. What must each person do in
order to understand what God has done (verse 16)?

9. What is present with the Spirit of the Lord (verse 17)?

Do you often associate freedom with being in God's will?
Why or why not?

♦ **10.** What becomes of us as we reflect God's glory? In contrast to the world molding you, what does it mean to you to be transformed by the Spirit? Have you experienced this? How?

If our faces are reflecting the glory of God, what must we be looking at?

11. After reviewing these verses, what do you see that you must *do* in order to do God's will? On his part, what does *God* do in order that you may do his will?

12. How is the process of fulfilling Paul's three instructions working out in your life? Is there a next step you should be taking or a new insight you should apply to your life now? Pray about this and write down your answer. Then pray for God's help to do it.

GOD'S WILL AND THE BIBLE

Joshua 1:1-9; 2 Timothy 3:14-17

We've all heard the story about the person whose plan for Bible reading was to close his eyes, open the book, put his finger on a spot, and read it. One day his finger fell on the verse that read, "and Judas went out and hanged himself." Puzzled as to how he could apply such a verse as God's will for the day, the reader closed his eyes, opened to another page, and read, "Go now, and do likewise."

As we'll discover in this study, one way of learning God's will for us is applying his Word to our lives. But *applying* God's Word is something we must also learn. Following are some foundations for using the Bible in this task.

1. What is your usual method for discovering God's will for you through the Bible?

Read Joshua 1:1-9.

◆ **2.** The Lord was encouraging and instructing Joshua as he took over the leadership of the Israelites, following Moses' death. As they were about to enter the promised land, what specific instructions did God give to Joshua, and what active responses would this have called for on Joshua's part?

3. From these instructions, how would Joshua have felt he should use the Scriptures? How might he have been tempted to turn from the Law?

4. What do God's instructions to Joshua suggest about the way you should respond to the Scripture? What kind of prosperity and good success should you expect as a result?

5. Think about verse 9. What is the most helpful idea there for you right now?

6. What does it mean to "meditate" on God's law, and how should that affect the way you apply God's Word today?

Read 2 Timothy 3:14-17.

7. What kind of background has Timothy had that is advantageous for him? What part has Scripture played in his life thus far (verse 15)?

◆ **8.** Paul describes several functions performed in our lives by Scripture. What are they, in your own words?

When and how have you seen this at work in your own experience?

In what ways do you see yourself becoming more "equipped" for good works?

◆ **9.** What do you think is meant by the term "God-breathed"?

10. Paul was confident in Timothy's spiritual development partly because of Timothy's background; he had known and read Scripture for a long time. How might length of exposure to the Bible affect the way a Christian understands and applies its teachings?

Have you noticed any difference between how new Christians and more experienced Christians understand the Bible? If so, what are they?

If a person does not have extensive Bible background, what suggestions might you make regarding his or her spiritual growth?

11. In summary, what are some specific ways you should act on what you know of God's will from Scripture? How should you seek to acquire additional and deeper understanding of God's will from Scripture?

GOD'S WILL AND THE UNKNOWN

Proverbs 16:1-9; Romans 15:30-32

Just a quick glance at television commercials will indicate the average person's interest in the unknown. Personal psychics are just a phone call away, ready to supply information on your love life, financial security, and your lucky numbers. Even those people who have no confidence in so-called supernatural information systems will tune in to the latest from environmental and economic experts. We want to know what is going to happen to us.

The Bible is not a book of magic, and those who try to use it as such will only be disappointed. But God's Word gives us important information on how to live and how to deal effectively with situations that we don't yet know about.

1. How can a person have hope in an uncertain world? As a Christian, what can you confidently assert about the future?

Read Proverbs 16:1-9.

2. Of all biblical books, Proverbs is probably the most pragmatic in its approach to life. It is a collection of sayings about wisdom and foolishness, how to succeed and how to fail. What does this passage say about humankind's ability to predict the future?

What is our best protection in light of life's uncertainty?

♦ **3.** Verse 5 says that God "detests all the proud of heart . . ." What attitude toward future and destiny would you consider to be proud?

4. What role do we play in our own future, according to verses 3 and 9?

5. According to verse 6, how do we receive forgiveness and avoid evil?

What kind of guidance can we find in helping us attain faithfulness, love, and fear of the LORD?

6. What else must we do, according to verse 7, in order for life to go better for us?

7. Proverbs 19:21 says that "many are the plans in a man's heart, but it is the LORD's purpose that prevails."

Where do we find what God's purposes are?

8. These verses in Proverbs assume that we can under-stand what pleases God and can maintain a lifestyle to which God will respond favorably by taking ultimate con-trol of our future. How can we learn to live in a way that pleases God, and where can we find principles for a life-style that will find God's blessing?

Jesus Christ had commissioned Paul to carry his name "before the Gentiles and their kings and before the people of Israel" (Acts 9:15). Paul had a job to complete and was used to decision making and quick action. In the follow-ing verses we see some indication of Paul's attitude toward "God's will" in the directing of his ministry.

"But I will come to you very soon, if the Lord is will-ing . . ."—1 Corinthians 4:19

"I hope to spend some time with you, if the Lord permits. But I will stay on at Ephesus until Pentecost, because a great door for effective work has opened to me . . ."
—1 Corinthians 16:7-9

"I will come back if it is God's will."—Acts 18:21

"I pray that now at last by God's will the way may be opened for me to come to you."—Romans 1:10

9. What do you think Paul means by the phrase "if God wills"? In what ways does Paul see God's will making a difference in the direction of his ministry?

In what specific ways was Paul expecting God to direct his movements and his ministry?

Read Romans 15:30-32.

◆ **10.** What part does prayer play in God's will? Why would prayer be such an urgent necessity in bringing about the will of a God who is almighty and sovereign?

What does Paul seem to be sure of, if anything, in these verses? What does he admit as being unknown to him?

11. What emphases do you see in these prayers of Paul that you should be applying to your own prayers?

What principles do you discover in these verses that you can apply in your own planning?

12. Does your attitude toward God's part in the direction of your life need to be revised after considering these passages? Have your expectations of the way God works been accurate or inaccurate? What examples can you remember to illustrate this?

THE HOLY SPIRIT'S GUIDANCE, 1

Galatians 5:16-26; Philippians 4:4-7

What does it mean to "walk by the Spirit"? Some people believe it implies a supernatural type of existence, complete with voices telling us what to do and when. Others assume that the Holy Spirit becomes part and parcel with our natural thought processes. Clearly, a person who lives by the Spirit should be different from one who does not have the Holy Spirit. But such a life is not automatic; we must participate in the changes God wants to make in us.

1. How is the work of the Holy Spirit evident to you in your inner life?

Read Galatians 5:16-26.

2. Contrast the kind of behavior produced by the "sinful nature" and the "spiritual nature" in the Christian.

3. In the world around us, which works of the flesh do people tend to oppose and which do they tolerate? Likewise, which fruits of the Spirit are valued and which ignored? What reactions do you find *you* have toward the characteristics described in these contrasting lists?

4. Who performs the "crucifying of the sinful nature" in verse 24? How is it done?

♦ **5.** What does it mean to "keep in step with the Spirit," (verse 25)?

6. Explain, from the Galatians passage, why victory is possible for the Christian in the battle between the natural (carnal) and spiritual.

7. What must you do for the Holy Spirit to enable you to walk in God's ways, producing his fruit mentioned in verses 22-23?

What fruit of the Spirit do you most need in *your* life?
What are some ways you find the Holy Spirit already
changing your old "works" to his "fruit"?

Read Philippians 4:4-7.

8. By what steps may we overcome anxiety? Think about
a specific situation that produces fear in you, then explain
how you would handle it if you were following Paul's
advice.

9. Why is it possible for Christians to rejoice? How can
this become a consistent reaction in any situation?

10. Have you ever experienced "the peace of God?" How would you describe it? In verse 7, what is the significance of the word "guard" in regard to the peace God gives?

11. What are some examples of finding this peace in difficult circumstances in your own life? In situations where you were making decisions?

12. Our Lord is a God of order, not confusion. Compulsive behavior or feelings of great anxiety are likely to spring from within ourselves or our circumstances rather than from the Lord. This week, as you encounter people or circumstances that make you anxious or confused, refer back to this study's Scripture passages—Galatians 5:16-26 and Philippians 4:4-7. Apply them, in prayer, to yourself and record the results.

THE HOLY SPIRIT'S GUIDANCE, 2

Selections from the book of Acts; James 3:13-18

"God is speaking all the time, all the time, all the time." (Frank Laubach)

Rosalind Rinker reflects on Dr. Laubach's words: "If God is speaking all the time, what am I doing all that time?

"I want to be listening all the time, all the time, all the time. I'm really no longer afraid, but I'm willing to listen because I'm absolutely convinced of God's great, never-changing, unconditional love for me, through Jesus Christ.

"The little things, the day-by-day things, our comings and goings, our hurts and our disappointments, our friends and loved ones, little children, flowers, trees, what we read, how we spend our money, what we do with our leisure time—through everything God has something to say to us."

Communicating Love through Prayer, Zondervan, 1966

1. What does it mean to you to listen to God? To listen *all* the time? What prevents most of us from doing this?

2. Paul experienced supernatural guidance a number of times as recorded in the New Testament. Look at the following examples, and answer these questions for each passage:

When did Paul experience these unusual means of guidance?

What kinds of guidance experiences were they?

What information was given to him?

Was he seeking this guidance?

Acts 13:1-4a

Acts 16:6-10

Acts 18:9-11

Acts 20:22-23

Acts 22:17-21

Acts 23:11

Acts 27:21-26

◆ **3.** Do you think you should seek "unusual" guidance today? Should you expect it? What should be your attitude regarding this kind of guidance?

4. What has God been teaching *you* about walking in the Spirit and listening to Him?

Read James 3:13-18.

5. What are the general characteristics of God's wisdom?

6. What are the general characteristics of wisdom that is not from God?

7. List some principles that can help you discern between choices inspired by the Holy Spirit and those coming from wrong or unwise sources.

GOD'S GUIDANCE AND PERSONAL PREFERENCE

2 Samuel 7:1-3, 5-7, 12-13; 1 Thessalonians 2:17–3:3

A popular Christian song begins, "Please don't send me to Africa."

Many Christians struggle with the idea that what they really want in life will surely not be in God's will for them. This attitude has grown out of a view that sees pleasure of any kind as somehow wrong and elevates sacrifice above joy.

To be sure, whatever God "calls" us to do in life, we can never know ahead of time the trials and suffering that will come with it. *Every* Christian's path in life will involve some suffering and sacrifice, because the pioneer of our faith, Jesus Christ, suffered and sacrificed. But even Jesus had preferences—of where to go and who to see. Sometimes his plans got changed, but that didn't prevent him from acting on his own preferences and good motives. In this study, we see how King David and the apostle Paul followed good inclinations and trusted God to aid or intervene in the carrying out of plans.

1. What are your deepest desires in life? Is there anything wrong with these desires, and, if so, how can you reshape them to fit God's purposes?

Read 2 Samuel 7:1-3, 5-7, 12-13.

2. What was David's desire? How did the prophet Nathan respond to David's wish?

3. How did God intervene and why?

Did God change David's plans because they were not good plans or because God had another method of carrying them out? Explain.

♦ **4.** The follow-up to this story is found in 1 Kings 8:10-19.
David's son, Solomon, is now king and the temple has
been built and dedicated. Solomon makes a speech in
which he states, "My father David had it in his heart to
build a temple for the Name of the LORD, the God of
Israel. But the LORD said to my father David, 'Because it
was in your heart to build a temple for my Name, you did
well to have this in your heart. Nevertheless, you are not
the one to build the temple . . .' " What does this statement say about the plans we make?

♦ **5.** Think through some plans you have had that were not
carried out for some reason. List a few that were good
plans—for good actions and with good motives. Imagine
God saying to you what he said to David: "You did well
to have this in your heart." How can this change the emotions you feel that are connected with that "failed" plan?

Read 1 Thessalonians 2:17–3:3.

◆ **6.** Paul's visit to the Thessalonians had been a short one. When the unbelieving Jews caused a city riot the Christian believers had to send Paul away for his own safety. This is a letter he wrote shortly afterwards. What had Paul tried to do more than once? What emotions were present in Paul's life during this time?

◆ **7.** Who did Paul blame for his plans not coming to pass?

How did Paul readjust his plans?

What kind of emotions did Paul experience that led him to make alternate plans?

8. Think of a time when good plans of yours were thwarted. How did you deal with it? Did you make different plans according to the circumstances? What did you do, and how did the situation turn out?

9. Looking at this passage, what would you say were the driving desires—concerns—in Paul's life?

Did these overall desires coincide with God's will?

10. What are your *overall* desires for life? In what ways are they consistent with what God wants in the world?

In what ways are they not consistent, if any?

11. What has been your attitude about considering your desires when trying to discern God's will?

12. Look at just one of your overall desires and list a variety of ways in which that desire could be carried out. Pray about this desire, and acknowledge to God that these are the best plans you have, but he may have a better way. Ask for patience and wisdom as you feel your way through the fulfillment of this desire.

GOD'S GUIDANCE AND GOOD SENSE

1 Corinthians 16:1-12; Daniel 1:1-17

Have you ever heard the phrase, "You're too heavenly minded to be of any earthly good"? The Christian who puts too much emphasis on the merely supernatural workings of God and ignores the down-to-earth details of daily life can give others the impression that he or she is not well equipped in areas of common sense or intellectual development. Since the Pietist movement in the 17th and 18th centuries, large segments of the Christian community have rejected development of intellect as a reaction to the Age of Reason that displaced God as the center of the universe and put human intellect in that position.

Yet God created the human mind, along with its unbelievable capacity to process information and do its own creating in the environment. At times we focus only on the "supernatural" in the lives of God's people, when the power of the intellect is itself a miracle. Following is a look at some *overlooked* aspects of guidance in the lives of Paul and Daniel.

1. In what ways is intellect helpful to spiritual growth and direction? In what ways can it be a detriment?

Read 1 Corinthians 16:1-12.

2. What areas of church life are addressed in this passage?

What general principles of money management—and human nature—underlie Paul's instructions on the collection of church funds?

3. On what information did Paul base his travel plans?

What were the reasons behind some of those plans?

4. What phrase or phrases indicate that Paul acknowledged God's involvement in his plans and appointments?

5. What phrase or phrases indicate that Paul took much
responsibility for figuring out situations and options for
himself?

Read Daniel 1:1-17.

◆ **6.** What attributes did Daniel already have when he was
chosen to be trained for the king's service (verses 3-4)?

7. Verse 9 says that "God had caused the official to show favor and sympathy to Daniel." Why was this not enough to convince the official to let Daniel stay within Hebrew dietary laws (verse 10)?

8. What ploy did Daniel use to enable him to stay within God's laws? How was this action well within "reasonable" means?

9. Daniel becomes known for the several supernatural interventions in his life, including his ability to interpret dreams. What other abilities in Daniel's development are attributed to God (verse 17)?

10. Circumstances and educational opportunities prepared Paul and Daniel for the jobs God gave to them. What does this say to you about your own past experience?

11. Do some brainstorming in the following areas of your own life:

Past training and present opportunities

Special interests and areas of expertise

Principles of logic, finance, business, and other areas that can be applied to "spiritual" areas of life

12. We find Paul and Daniel trusting God and using all the resources at hand, including human intelligence, to accomplish the tasks God had given them. To scan either one of their stories reveals men who were bold and free in their approaches to life. Is there anything revealed in this study that offers you new hope and freedom as you seek to live God's will? Explain.

GOD'S GUIDANCE AND CIRCUMSTANCES

Acts 24:22-27; Philippians 1:12-14; Matthew 14:6-21

Sometimes the events of our lives seem hopelessly out of control. At face value, Paul's arrest and imprisonment were a bureaucratic nightmare and the miscarriage of justice, but Paul and others saw another side to his circumstances. The story is a prime example of God's guidance.

Although we tend to think of Jesus as being above his circumstances, he subjected himself to the same forces of time and place that confront all humans. Often he found himself in precarious circumstances, but he proved that people who are walking in God's Spirit can have authority even over the outcome of events that are seemingly out of our control.

1. How have you used circumstances in your determination of God's will for you? How has your method worked? What questions do you still have about this area of guidance?

Read Acts 24:22-27.

2. At the close of Paul's third missionary journey, he
arrived in Jerusalem. Here, though innocent, he was
arrested by Roman soldiers, and eventually taken to Felix,
the governor. What ministry opportunity did Paul have
during this time? What was the potential of this opportunity?

3. In Acts 28:30-31 we see Paul during this imprisonment:
"For two whole years Paul stayed there in his own rented
house and welcomed all who came to see him. Boldly and
without hindrance he preached the kingdom of God and
taught about the Lord Jesus Christ." How were God's purposes accomplished in these circumstances?

4. In terms of justice, Paul's imprisonment was unfair and
uncalled for. What types of situations have you experienced that were not fair, nevertheless God's purposes
were carried out? Explain.

Read Philippians 1:12-14.

5. How did Paul view his situation?

How did he make use of his circumstances?

How might Paul have experienced God's strength in his circumstances?

6. What kinds of things are *automatically* "God's will" for you because of the circumstances of your life? What things are *not* God's will, regardless of your circumstances? What things *are* God's will, regardless of your circumstances?

Read Matthew 14:6-21.

◆ **7.** What prompted Jesus to withdraw from the crowds and head out across the lake?

What do you think he was planning to do?

8. When Jesus landed on the other side of the lake, what did he find? How did he react?

9. What problem presented itself as evening came? What could be the outcome of these circumstances—a huge crowd of people and nothing to eat? What *was* the outcome of these events?

10. As the disciples observed their weary, grieving teacher ministering to the crowd, what might they have been learning? What would they learn from the miracle of the food?

11. When have you experienced a change of circumstances that at first seemed "bad" but turned out quite differently? What happened?

Can you think of a time when circumstances changed the direction of your actions? Describe the event.

12. What place should circumstances have in an individual's life, particularly as he or she seeks to know God's will? What danger is involved in reading too much into circumstances? What danger is involved in ignoring circumstances?

GOD'S GUIDANCE AND HUMAN COUNSEL

Acts 15:1-35; 2 Chronicles 10:1-19

We have more channels of advice open to us than ever. There are financial advisers for our money matters, therapists for our inner battles, consultants for our businesses, counselors for our marriages, and pastors for our spiritual needs. Where does any or all of it figure into God's will?

Actually, the Bible conveys a high view of finding and listening to wise counsel. The pastoral letters we find in the New Testament are full of counsel to young believers and churches. In this study we will look closely at two examples of counseling at work and how it can affect our lives—for better or worse.

1. Who, if anyone, do you consult when you are in the process of making a major decision?

Read Acts 15:1-35.

2. What controversy threatened to tear the Christians apart?

3. What did the church leaders do to solve this problem?

4. What took place in the decision-making process among the elders from Antioch and those in Jerusalem?

What part did Scripture play in this process?

What part did personal experience and testimony play?

5. How was this issue resolved?

◆ **6.** What actions and/or attitudes could have prevented the elders from arriving at an agreed-upon decision?

What attitudes made way for a decision to be reached?

Who was the final authority in these deliberations?

Read 2 Chronicles 10:1-19.

7. The new king Rehoboam had a problem; what was it?

How did he seek to solve this problem?

◆ **8.** What did the elders have to say to the king?

For whom did the elders serve as counselors in the past, and what might that say about their credentials?

9. What did the young men who had grown up with Rehoboam say?

Regardless of who gave what advice, which mode of action sounds wisest to you, and why?

10. Why might Rehoboam have been hesitant to accept the elders' advice?

Why do you think he accepted the counsel of the younger men?

◆ **11.** How does this story end? What does it reveal about how to seek counsel and who to listen to?

12. Can you think of a time when you took another person's advice mainly because he or she agreed with your viewpoint and not so much because the counsel itself was wise? Explain the situation.

What other factors can prevent us from recognizing wise counsel?

13. Make a list of what you consider necessary qualities for a counselor. Sketch out how you would go about receiving counsel in a specific situation, like deciding on which job to take or which ministry to be involved in.

GOD'S GUIDANCE AND SOVEREIGNTY

Acts 4:23-31; Nehemiah 2:1-8

Since God gives all people the freedom to choose, how can God possibly exercise any control over the world? How can we be sure that God's will can and will be done on earth? And how are we to pray and act in light of events we can't predict? What can we hope for?

The very first church faced these questions early on, but they weren't the first people to marvel at God's sovereignty in an uncertain world. This study looks at the early Christians as well as a leader in Israel's ancient history, Nehemiah, who discovered step by step that God still had control of people's destinies.

1. How do you pray when you are in the midst of turmoil and confusion?

Read Acts 4:23-31.

2. Peter and John have been brought before the Sanhedrin and told that they must not preach in Jesus' name anymore. Yet Peter and John replied that they must obey God, not people. What did Peter and John—and the rest of the believers—expect was going to happen to them?

How did this affect their willingness to preach and teach about Jesus?

3. How did the Christians see God's hand at work in regard to leaders and governments?

What did they trust God to do?

4. In their prayer, what did Peter and John ask the Lord to do? Did they have any reason to believe that they would be spared persecution? Explain your answer.

What would you have requested in such a situation? How does your concept of God's sovereignty compare with that expressed here by early Christians?

5. How was their prayer answered? What kind of answers can you expect from God when you are doing his work in his way?

6. How does a realization of God's sovereignty help you to develop a proper concept of "God's guidance"?

Read Nehemiah 2:1-8.

♦ **7.** Nehemiah, an exiled Jew, was in the city of Susa in the land of Persia. He became distressed when he heard of the desperate situation back in Jerusalem, and mourned for days, fasting and praying for his people. He prayed specifically for success and mercy from the king. In this narrative, what were Nehemiah's *feelings* and *actions?*

In what ways is he a good example for us?

8. How do you see the "good hand" of God upon Nehemiah in this situation?

9. In both the situations of Peter and John and of Nehemiah, what kind of risks had to be taken in order to see God's sovereignty?

What kinds of expectations did Nehemiah and the Christians in Acts have about their situations?

◆ **10.** Write out your own definition of God's sovereignty in light of these passages. How does God's sovereignty involve more than merely influencing circumstances?

What is required in our relationship with God if we are to fully appreciate the sovereignty of God?

TRUSTING GOD FOR GUIDANCE

Proverbs 3:5-8; 2 Chronicles 20:5-12; John 10:2-18

Ralph Waldo Emerson wrote, "All I have seen teaches me to trust the Creator for all I have not seen." And Jean Paul Richter said, "How calmly we may commit ourselves to the hands of him who bears up the world." Here are two glimpses of trust that can encourage us in any circumstances. Rather than trying to figure out how God is going to guide us and what is going to happen, we are much better off trusting in the *character* of the One who created the world. In the end, we trust God in much the same way that we trust another person; the more we know who God is, the easier it becomes to put all things in his care.

1. What are some synonyms for *trust*? How do we come to trust another? How much depends on the one we trust, and how much depends on our trust in that one?

Read Proverbs 3:5-8.

2. The word "acknowledge" means "to know." What does it mean to *know* God in all your ways?

3. According to this passage, what results show up in a life that is lived in this kind of trust? Are they evident in your life? Why or why not?

4. What are we *not* to do? How would this affect our living?

5. How can this kind of trust "bring health to your body and nourishment to your bones"?

What effects do stress and anxiety have on us physically?

6. Is it enough to "fear the Lord"? What else is included in that command (verse 7)?

What does this say about *our* responsibility in living life in God's will?

Read 2 Chronicles 20:5-12.

7. The nation of Judah was in a difficult situation. Jehoshaphat, their king, had called the nation to fast and seek the Lord. For what did the king pray?

8. What actions of God in the past gave Jehoshaphat the confidence to ask for help now?

Why did Jehoshaphat feel justified in praying for protection (verses 10-11)?

9. What was the people's relationship to God as expressed in the prayer? How would you describe their attitude at the conclusion of their prayer?

Read John 10:2-18.

10. What does Jesus say in this passage that is encouraging to you, and why?

11. Jesus acknowledges that others will try to lead us, others whose motives are harmful. Why is Jesus confident that his "sheep" will not follow another "shepherd"?

What is the significance of the statement: "I know my sheep and my sheep know me"?

12. What are Jesus' motives as a shepherd?

◆ **13.** Based on the passages of this study, what encouraging things can you tell yourself in times of trouble and confusion?

Whose decision must it be to follow God?

Whose responsibility is it to care for those who have decided to follow?

Pray together to recommit yourselves to following God and listening and looking for his guidance.

LEADER'S NOTES

Question 3. Paul says, "Therefore, I urge you, brothers, in view of God's mercy . . ." In the last verses of Romans 11, he has outlined the goodness of God. He has just finished explaining what the Christian has through God's grace. The logic in Romans 12 is that we have received so much from God, the least we can do is give our lives back to God—lives we wouldn't even have if it were not for his mercy and love.

Question 7. The emphasis in both the Hebrew and Greek words for *will* is, that which is one's "good pleasure"; not so much a legalistic purpose or plan, but that in which one delights.

Question 8. In these verses *veil* refers to people's inability to see God's grace or understand it. When Moses came down from the mountain after talking with God, his face shone with God's glory so much that he had to cover it with a veil. Similarly, a "veil" covers the mystery of salvation, and only Christ can take the veil away so that we can understand it (2 Corinthians 3:14).

Question 10. The same Greek word is used for "conformed to this world" (Romans 12:2) and "transformed into his (Christ's) likeness."

▪ Study 2/God's Will and the Bible

Question 2. The "law of Moses" referred to here is comprised of the first five books of the Old Testament.

Question 8. *Teaching* is self explanatory; *rebuking* involves letting us know when we are on the wrong track; *correcting* helps us to change our ways back to the right track; *training in righteousness* goes further than teaching—it has to do with equipping us to do all that God has for us to do for the kingdom.

Question 9. The Bible is not just a human book. Through the process known as "inspiration," the Holy Spirit revealed God's message to human authors. Though they wrote from their own personal, historical, and cultural contexts, God was in control of the writing. Since the Scriptures are "God-breathed," they are completely trustworthy and authoritative for our faith and our lives.

▪ Study 3/God's Will and the Unknown

Question 3. For a passage that speaks explicitly to this, see James 4:13-17.

Question 10. Although God has the power to do anything in the world, he chose to give people freedom of choice. Therefore, a lot of things that happen in the world are clearly *not* God's will, because God will not prevent our actions nor reverse their consequences. In Romans 15:30 Paul speaks of others joining in his *struggle* and praying to God for him. Obviously, God's will does not automatically happen even in the lives of believing Christians. Jesus warned Peter in Luke 22:31 that Satan was going to test him, and his prayer for the disciples in John 17 included requests for their care in a world that was quite opposed to all they stood for. Ephesians 6 speaks explicitly of a spiritual warfare that engages our constant attention. God's will is brought about by our own choices, by our battle against evil, and by God's grace and providence. The Lord's Prayer asks God to protect us from evil and to steer us away from temptation. But God will not *force* us from where we choose to go. The apostle Paul was often in the middle of volatile situations, and he needed constant prayer so that he would respond to his opponents wisely. He was no doubt tempted to be angry on a regular basis, and, while he acknowledged that he desired to do worthy things, like visit believers, he also knew that desire does not always lead us in the best direction at the time.

◼ Study 4/The Holy Spirit's Guidance, 1

Question 5. "In justification (the single act of our redemption) the instrument by which we receive the free gift of God is faith, which believes God as he has given us his promises in the Bible. In sanctification (the Christian's lifelong process of growth) the instrument by which we receive the free gift of God is faith, which believes God as he has given us his promises in the Bible. It is exactly the same thing" (Frances Schaeffer, *True Spirituality*, p. 85. Wheaton, Ill.: Tyndale House Publishers, 1979).

◼ Study 5/The Holy Spirit's Guidance, 2

Question 3. We should be cautious about seeking "unusual" guidance. Looking for it could lead to self-deception or neglect of other means of guidance God has provided. But we must realize that

God can give extraordinary guidance to his children when he knows it is necessary.

The secret of "inner" guidance lies in finding a balance between a search for unusual guidance and learning to "hear" God through whatever means he may use to communicate to us, be it in Scripture, inner convictions, or circumstances.

God's guidance has definite characteristics that are in keeping with God's character. His voice has a simplicity and rightness to it. He doesn't manipulate people with threats, fear, or condemnation. There is usually adequate time to carry out his directions. Confusion and anxiety are often indications that the voice we hear is not the Lord's.

Sometimes, if we are not sure, we must wait and watch, asking God to reinforce his directions or give us a settled peace about a decision we are making.

■ Study 6/God's Guidance and Personal Preference

Question 4. Many good plans are made, but not all of them are carried out. Even though we have good ideas, sometimes there are better ones that need to supersede them. But notice that God was not unhappy with David for these plans; in fact, he was pleased with David's motives.

Question 5. We must accept that a plan's not turning out doesn't mean that we were wrong to think of it or try to do it. We often confuse success with God's will: if something succeeds, it must have been God's will—when in actuality, some evil plans succeed, and some good plans haven't come into their time yet or are simply prevented.

Question 6. Some plans don't come to fruition because they are interrupted by people and events that are in opposition to God's will.

It is difficult to say why God allows good plans to be thwarted. Romans 8:28 asserts that God will make even bad situations bear good results, and we must learn to count on this principle when the situation turns bleak.

Question 7. It's important to note that Paul was not free of anxiety and emotional pain during this time. The idea that a Christian in God's will does not suffer emotionally is unfounded in Scripture. Some people assume that their anxiety and "lack of peace" are indications that they are doing the wrong thing or in the wrong place. Sometimes this is the case, but certainly not always.

■ Study 7/God's Guidance and Good Sense

Question 6. Background and training play important roles in our life plans under God's direction. The apostle Paul (in the previous study passage) grew up in the capital of Cilicia, Tarsus, a thriving commercial center and university town. In this Hellenistic environment he would have been influenced by the order and prosperity of Roman political control. Paul was a Jew, raised in the customs and manners of his people. Paul was also a Roman citizen by inheritance, which, on occasion, provided physical protection. His religious training was that of a Pharisee and took place in Jerusalem under the direction of the famous Gamaliel. Thus Paul was a student of the Jewish Law. By trade he was a tentmaker (all rabbis had a trade by which they supported themselves.). With this background Paul would know Greek, the language of his Hellenistic hometown; Aramaic, the language of Judea; Hebrew, the language used in his scribal studies, and Latin the language of Rome. His culture was that of Israel, Greece, and Rome, making it easier for him to "be all things to all people," as he said was a necessity in the preaching of the gospel.

The same kind of preparation was true in the case of Daniel, a youth who rose to positions of power in Babylon and was used time and again as God's intermediary. Daniel was a son of royalty, physically and mentally gifted. Another example of God using our attributes for purposes of a larger scheme is Esther, the Hebrew girl who was so attractive that she was chosen to be queen of a foreign ruler (Esther 2:1-18). Because of her connections to her own people as well as the king, she was able to save the Israelites from genocide.

■ Study 8/God's Guidance and Circumstances

Question 7. John the Baptist was Jesus' cousin, and the first one who recognized Jesus as God's chosen one. John's ministry was to be a forerunner of Jesus. Thus, they had not only family ties but close ties of ministry and destiny. Jesus was obviously grieved to hear of John's death and sought some time to himself.

■ Study 9/God's Guidance and Human Counsel

Question 6. The Holy Spirit became the authority, along with God's written Word, because the signs and miracles that had been experienced could not be denied, and all assumed the authority of the prophecy quoted in Acts 15:16-17.

Question 8. These elders had been Solomon's counselors, and Solomon was and is considered one of the wisest men to have ever lived and ruled in Israel. This doesn't guarantee that Solomon's elders would give fool-proof advice, but they were certainly worthy to receive a serious hearing.

Question 11. 2 Chronicles 10:16-19 records the beginning of the divided kingdom. Rehoboam lost the chance to rule a peaceful, united kingdom as his father Solomon had. Now the kingdom divided into two parts: Ten of the tribes followed Jeroboam, calling their nation Israel, or the northern kingdom. The other two tribes became Judah, or the southern kingdom, under Rehoboam's rule.

■ Study 10/God's Guidance and Sovereignty

Question 7. "The sorry state of Jerusalem is a direct consequence of Artaxerxes' decree that building should cease (Ezra 4:7-23). Nehemiah therefore takes his life in his hands in championing a city which has been represented to the king as a hot-bed of rebellion. Even by letting his grief show in the king's presence he places himself in grave danger. But Nehemiah's concern for his people outweighs self-interest" *(Eerdman's Handbook to the Bible,* p. 309. Grand Rapids, Mich.: William B. Eerdmans Publishing Company, 1973).

Question 10. Those who trust God's sovereignty are usually trusting God's hand in the bigger picture rather than in details; they also commit themselves to the ways of God, recognizing that consequences are not always pleasant. They put God's larger purposes in front of their own desires and needs.

■ Study 11/Trusting God for Guidance

Question 13. Encourage group members to write a summary on God's will and guidance, with a short statement from each study of this studyguide. Write it in such a way that you can refer to it quickly as a reference when you are in the midst of decision-making and hard situations.

WHAT SHOULD WE STUDY NEXT?

To help your group answer that question, we've listed the Fisherman Guides by category so you can choose your next study.

TOPICAL STUDIES

BIBLE BOOK STUDIES

Genesis, Fromer & Keyes

Job, Klug

Psalms, Klug

Proverbs: Wisdom That Works, Wright

Ecclesiastes, Brestin

Jonah, Habakkuk, & Malachi, Fromer & Keyes

Matthew, Sibley

Mark, Christensen

Luke, Keyes

John: Living Word, Kuniholm

Acts 1-12, Christensen

Paul (Acts 13-28), Christensen

Romans: The Christian Story, Reapsome

1 Corinthians, Hummel

Strengthened to Serve (2 Corinthians), Plueddemann

Galatians, Titus & Philemon, Kuniholm

Ephesians, Baylis

Philippians, Klug

Colossians, Shaw

Letters to the Thessalonians, Fromer & Keyes

Letters to Timothy, Fromer & Keyes

Hebrews, Hunt

James, Christensen

1 & 2 Peter, Jude, Brestin

How Should a Christian Live? (1, 2 & 3 John), Brestin

Revelation, Hunt

BIBLE CHARACTER STUDIES

Ruth & Daniel, Stokes

David: Man after God's Own Heart, Castleman

Job, Klug

King David: Trusting God for a Lifetime, Castleman

Elijah, Castleman

Men Like Us, Heidebrecht & Scheuermann

Peter, Castleman

Paul (Acts 13-28), Christensen

Great People of the Bible, Plueddemann

Women Like Us, Barton

Women Who Achieved for God, Christensen

Women Who Believed God, Christensen